Whale Fall

Whale Fall

POEMS

David Baker

W. W. NORTON & COMPANY
Independent Publishers Since 1923

Excerpt from "Cancer" from *Orphan Hours: Poems* by Stanley Plumly.
Copyright © 2012 by Stanley Plumly. Used by permission of W. W. Norton & Company, Inc.

Excerpt from "Slow Child with a Book of Birds" from *The Widening Leaves* by Larry Levis,
© 1991. Reprinted by permission of the University of Pittsburgh Press.

For information about permission to reproduce selections from this book, write to
Permissions, W. W. Norton & Company, Inc., 500 Fifth Avenue, New York, NY 10110

For information about special discounts for bulk purchases, please contact
W. W. Norton Special Sales at specialsales@wwnorton.com or 800-233-4830

Manufacturing by Versa Press
Production manager: Lauren Abbate

ISBN: 978-1-324-02063-9

W. W. Norton & Company, Inc.
500 Fifth Avenue, New York, N.Y. 10110
www.wwnorton.com

W. W. Norton & Company Ltd.
15 Carlisle Street, London W1D 3BS

1 2 3 4 5 6 7 8 9 0

for Page

Look how I am attached to the ends of things

Contents

ONE

The Telling   3

Mullein   4

Nineteen Spikes   8

Turner's Clouds for Plumly   11

Storm Psalm   15

Snow Falling   17

Is there no sound to   20

TWO

Middle Devonian   23

Sensationalism   27

Nine Wild Turkeys in a Field   30

Gravel 32

The Loneliness of Animals 34

Extinction 37

A slight wrinkle 39

THREE

Whale Fall 43

FOUR

Elegiac 61

A Portrait of My Father in Seven Maps 62

One September 66

Hold Hands 68

Six Hours 69

We Are Gone 71

We never ended 74

FIVE

Echolocation 77

This Morning 82

Four Poses 84

The Bathers at Nerja 86

Thirty-Six Silos   87

So Far   90

It doesn't take much   93

Acknowledgments   94

Notes   95

ONE

The Telling

Down from such heights and up from depths beyond
measure the old ice
than the stones can hold
the one note of a
in ages since we've
holds us in its heavy
now at the pace of
down the valley it
have stopped it is
almost there singing
the last time either

slowly now quicker
it knows its path like
bird flown beyond us
forgotten the wind
sleeves so sorry
our elders' tongues
is going the clocks
happy to be finished
the song no one heard
when the rains began.

Mullein

A single stalk
      by the side of the creek.
I put my hand in.
      Cold water the color of clouds.
Verbascum thapsus—
      it's what the book calls
subshrub, but not
      to be confused with moth
mullein, famous
      for its five antennae stamens
and branded noxious
      in some states nearby.
The common is
      uncommon. Like this one,
singular in a scuff
      of cinder and scratch grass
where the field runs
      down to sun-bruised stone,
where the creek
      grows narrow as it turns,
quicker over stones,
      clear white, like a covering.

What you call
      a thing is seldom what it is.

My father called
        his half-brother Buster.
His work friend
        Doc. His uncle-in-law Buddy.
And once, in an
        eddy pool under willow roots,
just there, a late Jurassic
        remnant he called *finger-*
snapper simmered
        in night shadow. We pulled it out
sleek and gray
        as a leg bone, a long-nosed
gar, caught on
        our bank line—fifty years ago,
more. But not to be
        confused with catfish,
carp, the needle
        snout three times longer
than its head,
        razor teeth jeweling the jaw.

Once the night
        was so long he carried me
back to camp, under
        starlight, under whippoorwills
calling, constant
        flutter of water over stones.
Durd's place, a
        friend's hundred acres of corn.

Carless Earl, some
        kind of cousin. The litany
of names in his
        stories—but not to be confused
with the ones
        he wouldn't name but to curse
a color. Lamb's ear,
        soft green-gray granular
texture of leaves, the sage-
        on-your-hands smell.
My friend writes
        the Amish girls rouged their cheeks
with mullein. Woolly
        mullein. Great mullein—

butter-colored
        flowers, a flannel softness.
Beggar's blanket. Names
        continuing through the night.
I have called out
        ugly things in my father's
fathers' anger. Dear
        mullein. Ancient jewel.
Burning teeth.
        I lean over shadows of
a billion years.
        I swirl the water
where it runs
        cold, until I can't feel my fingers.

Are you there?

      Farmer's bandage. Ghost-
in-shadows.

      Not to be confused—. Hag
taper. Garfish.

      Candlewick. I take my hand out.
I put it in again—.

Nineteen Spikes

Then the storm came. It raked our world with terrible teeth.
Then dissolved—like a calcium spike—back into bone—

I see what you mean. But your barn's not really a barn.
Old lady just sat there—married to the guy fifty years—

Wash your doorknob. Your hands. Triage your mail.
I had a nightmare I was living my present life—

Can't touch my nose. It's called *resorption*. What?
It throbs like crickets in my ears. Your BP was *what?*—

No touching. COVID petals. She said wash your hands.
It took his body hours to work down through the corn—

The quicksand weight of it. Her in her folding chair.
Him with a new auger for the bin. He sort of spilled out—

So the viburnum's full of little pink blooms. Bees in orbit.
With their spikes, their barbs—poisons—perfumes—

Then the hail balls, jagged as kidney stones, half a foot of rain.
Trees seemed to blow up—then the whole thing, whoosh—

Some natural forms are so successful they're viral.
Calcium nodes on your clavicle. I see them everywhere—

How small can they get? How big? Any size explodes—
Is it gas? You mean the barn? Is it gas? A heat storm—

Barn = a non-SI metric unit of area equal to 10^{-28} m² (or 100 fm²)—
To quantify interaction of a nucleus with an electric field gradient—

And branchlets are pithy, many-angled, winged. *Liquid-
Ambar styraciflua*. Surrounded by rusty, hairy bracts—

Looks like a tiny naval mine. Between 80 and 120 spikes.
Terminal barbs. A special form of moored contact mine—

And equipped with a plummet. He fell right through.
The spikes on the outer edge of the virus particles—

Give coronaviruses their name. Sweet gum. Storax.
Redgum. Star-leaved alligator-wood. Limpet mine—

In place of torpedoes, the silos carry twelve charges.
I heard my heartbeat in my bones. A positive "kill rate"—

Airbnb. *Missile Silo Fixer-Upper Now Swanky Bachelor Pad*.
Storm shelter; a storage bin; your "ultimate" safe room—

Each virus is a single pleomorphic spherical particle—
Satin-walnut—with bulbous surface projections—

I see what you mean. Wash your hands. Like that really helps.
Leaves ripped clean off. It's coming back. I know—

Turner's Clouds for Plumly

—Cloud cold sky. He was speaking of Turner,
though we had just turned the corner on Well Walk
and down the last cobbles to the Keats house,
its gray-white stone walls gathered like ground fog.
He had talked all day—painting to painting—
through one long room in London's National.
He bit into his beard to quiet now.
Tight grass. Cankered catalpa in half leaf.

In books he calls the paintings landscapes of
water, wild beyond human artifice.
They are what our feelings are without us.
They are, beyond us, peaceable masters—
in poem after poem on Keats, clouds,
then the talking essays, the cataloging
student in him calling forth poetry
even in the later prose. Of *The Sun*

of Venice Going to Sea—dark oil. It
is only a fishing boat, yet it casts
the larger spell of a vessel moving
in the direction of a destiny . . .
—We'd crossed the entry room and started toward
the cellar. It's what he wanted to see,
a breath of cloud as coal smoke in shadow.
Mary first, then Margaret, Stanley, and me,

descending. He touched her shoulder where
a wing would be, to steady her, or right
himself. He said he'd come to study soot
and size, the cellar smaller than the house,
the ways the old chute served the home. It was
like, he quieted again, a mother's
crawlway in a kitchen in Ohio.
Welded ductwork, a bucket of brushes.

Nor had he needed to see the paintings.
It was companionship he wanted, like
confirming the coal service of the cellar,
and to hear himself mumble, just there, look,
the tree—his finger brushing air—and one
diminished figure in red, lost almost
in the landscape of the place. There he is.
Turner seemed to him like Keats must have felt.

Yet it's Keats whose imagined every
step he traced, as though alongside the man
broaching "the thousand things"—Nightingales
and sleeplessness, dreams, poetry, whatnots . . .
One story goes, in his telling each time,
his melancholy knowingness, that Keats
was called by Dr.— over the heath
to speak with Coleridge, walking there as well.

He was *a loose, slack, and not well dressed youth,*
the older poet would write, though they spoke
only a minute or so. *There is death*
in that hand, I said to—, when Keats
was gone; yet this was, I believe, before
the consumption showed itself distinctly.
From the first two specks of lung-blood coughed up,
Keats knew "the colour. I cannot be deceived . . .

that drop is my death warrant;—I must die."
Stanley said his started at a distance
five hundred and twenty light-years away
and fell as stardust into his sleeping mouth.
We live in one time but think in another.
When he saw the paintings again, the cloud
symbols, the impressionist's weightless swirls,
he must have felt the same something airy

and ominous coming down, the way each
canvas is an art of premonition.
In love we open our mouth. In dying
we open it wider, saying, he wrote,
in your voice, come forth. We came back up then
to the Keats room full of books and letters,
then out into the low front lawn and air
of a big tree's down-pitched breaking bough

sick with wilt. No one knew the bird singing
there, nipping berries from the bush broadside
to the gate. Constant the love song. Chatter
and trill. It gorged and sang, lifted to land
again on a subsequent twig. *Sweetheart*,
he said, and he might have meant a brown-gray bird.
Or any number of us in his flock
of friendships. He might have meant his mother

always with him, in sorrow, or another,
like others before her—the devotions,
adorations, the students at his feet . . .
Or he might have meant a song floating somewhere
else from a high silver-midnight plane tree
outside, calling all night long, in his voice,
sweetheart. He called to Margaret in the dark,
the last night of his mortal darkness—

it was his favorite time, after all, night's
black bird, starling, or startling redwing with its
wing-top slash of yellow from the midnight
branches of a tree, calling all night long
and ready now to leave among the leaves.
Turner paints the clouds as though they are thoughts,
he said, of what's to come. We see the end.
No one could see it brewing there but him.

Storm Psalm

Dear darkness. Dear where we bow our heads in disbelief.
    Dear disbelief, hardly bow our heads and
hardly speak, so we sing, such words as darkness
    shows us how on days on end.
                 So I sing it is

not hopeless. Hurry hurry. Nor faithless—to stand
    without faith, keeping open—. Now another
so they say, thus the trees utterly are still, and the wind is,
    and what wings there are utterly still
                 in such limbs

darkened above the barn. Bow down, for this darkness
    now above cedars. Smell of mint and tincture of
torn wood-pulp, or was that the last time, yes it was.
    Take shelter, take now cover
                 so take nothing

when it is time, for ye need no Thing but—. So I say
    the mighty voice upon the waters is, glory thundereth.
Twists of ivy like leather scales along a body
    of the big limbs hanging, bearing hard
                 down, to break.

Older than a door, older than a holding hand. His voyce
    breaks Cedars: breaks Cedars. The last time,
now lie in the doorway, in the tub, lie down, cover
    us with blankets. Yes hurry. Dear

                        hurry. Dear

disbelief, Great are thy bowell-mercies Lord:
    after thy judgements—. Clap now a great wing
over the barn, the cedars, pelt now, rain now,
    or is that the last time coming wild,

                        stones against

every pane breaking, is it the last, hail now whose
    particles breaking through as little toads, silver
fishes, everywhere. Seek shelter—. What more
    do you need from me, it makes the

                        forrest bare: take

the little ones quickly, bow down, great whirlwind
    in grit, now ice, excreate of stone and leaf-shred sound
of howling birds, so I say it is not faithless to lie
    in the doorway going down without

                        faith, dear hurry

keeping open vigil at the site out of stillness out of
darkness now the sudden breaking down Dear wind—

Snow Falling

I aimed to
work all weekend. *Her teacups   tiny shoes like two thimbles.*
                    I had not been well for so long.
By the time I'd wired the backyard, the right tools, a

book of specs
laid out, its diagrams and directions—that I could choose
                    among such languages—it had started.
First as mist. As cold sheath. Less as falling than floating

against the gray sub-
lime of pines   *like a coat of what's-to-come.* A crackling among
                    high needles more static than
whisper. More shiver than chill. She wanted—who's

to say then, it's too
cold, little one, I'm not well, no, not just now—a place
                    to play in the yard. A slide,
a swing or two. Who can say what passes for health, when

you've been so long
fevered. I cut the A-frames to size. Measured. Marked off
                    spots to drill for the standing platform.
I sawed in a whiteout of sound but for talking to myself.

There were lilacs
willing to open their black buds, all along the slippery walk,
                               but no; black water in the creek
crusted at the banks. It was like singing, the days, I tell you,

but no, whatever song
there was was frost breaking over the grass. Wind leaning
                            against dark limbs. I worked the weekend
through. I raised the beams, and screwed them tight, and fixed

a slide so she could
play   *a swing set*   *a cradle of snow.*
                        A thing I made for her. And now,
it seems, for you, amid the world's broken and shining things.

Is there no sound to   *stopping is there no*

stopping first at night   *this fitful quiet*

to waken now to   *find such heavy snow*

where was nothing trees   *shattered and hear it*

nowhere cloud landscape   *of silence stopping*

through the night my sleep   *a dream of falling*

beyond anywhere   *you might be listening—*

TWO

Middle Devonian

You can't kill it, my
good neighbor
      tells me. He means the half
      acre of bamboo seeded

from waste run-
off from the
      new development—
      just beyond the woods, there, beyond

the creek bed. *Can't*
dig it out. Can't blast it out.
      And you can't hack it out with your machete
      or a big old chainsaw. No way.

But he'd rather
have the bamboo than all those houses
      going up. *Who are they?*
      Why'd they rip out

the beech trees
and bulldoze the pawpaws?
      Godawful houses.
      And then they planted trees, in rows!—can you

believe that?
We're walking the
        cold creek bed,
        looking for fossils, the coral, the hollow

stem-tubes,
from when this
        was all a salty shallow sea.
        He polishes them for

his grandkids. He
mounts the good ones, labels
        them—the brachiopods, the trilobites—
        like little jewels, like magic

lifted from the shale-
beds and sandstone
        of the creek. He's got his fingers in
        the water again. *This one here's a keeper.*

Goldringia cy-
clops, I think. Middle Devonian.
        It's got a gyroconic shell. That means
        the whorls don't touch. *Crenulate frills . . .*

it's a nautilid, not
an ammonoid.
        There's been an early freeze this
        week, a bit of snow, the remnant crust

upthrust and broken,
curling in sunshine

> here and there, in the mud.
> It's thin as good dishes.

Here's one for you.
You know the pawpaw's

> *science name?* He's moved into
> the rutted pathway, where kids from the houses

smear their loud four-wheelers.
Asimina triloba.

> *How's that for irony?*
> Then we're quiet for a while. Bird song

at the level of
the branches. Old language

> in the leaves—late wren?—not in a hurry, but
> stirring. So he says, *Go Bucks.*

What? *Just*
thinking about the fires

> *out west. I read they're burning like eighty*
> *football fields of prairie*

every single minute.
What the hell

> *kind of way is that to measure something?*
> Beats me—. *I guess*

it's how they think
we understand the size.

      I can tell he's ready to leave.
      People round here love their trucks and football.

He pats his pocket
full of rocks—keepers for
      the kids. *Go Bucks*, he says again.
      Godawful. Think of that. One minute

and it's four hundred million years.

Sensationalism

This life & no other so says the news.
So says upright in the darkness my friend.
In his chair in the dark in his terrible year.
So the sage-green spurge we called blackbird,
discovered first as a sport, out of red wing,
hybrid *Euphorbia*, that has spread its brume
carpet like shadow beyond the barn, is the life
of the grass, though my three deer won't
go there, not until quietly the shadows grow
    long enough to nibble or lie down in.

2.

I would lie down to show him, even here.
Mice bones melting in downfall, in leaf-
mulch—I would tell him I did as he said.
Uprooted. Left to find this life & no other,
like flesh that has stepped out of its flesh.
It's got flowers, come spring, yellow-green
in bracts. It's got red stems. And it weeps,
says the book, a white sap, rather like latex.
And the lives in a book of extinct birds
    seem clearer than my own, as he says—.

3.

Today a band of ranchers, *we are not*
a militia, let's call them what they are, little
terrors, *it's getting dark, it's freezing,*
overtook, armed, a sanctuary for birds.
To protest, what? Flesh so innocent it walks
along the road, believing it, & ceases
to be ours? Listen. The average lifespan
of a species is ten million years, give or take.
Is the Snowy Egret extinct by now?
  Or does it only sound as if it is?

4.

The sedges were full of birds, the waters were
full of birds: avocets, stilts, willets, killdeers,
coots, phalaropes, rails, tule wrens, yellow-
headed black birds, black terns . . . 1914.
Dallas Lore Sharp went down to Lake Malheur.
Farallon cormorants, great white
pelicans, great glossy ibises, California gulls,
eared grebes, Western grebes—clouds of them,
acres of them, square miles—one hundred
  and forty-three square miles of them!

5.

This song and no other. Listen.
Staccato call of the greater sandhill crane.
It spreads its notes like shadow over the arms
of men. I would lie down, even there, if I could—.
If my friend would sit up suddenly, again—.
If the blackbird spurge, once a sport
out of red wing—. If the lonely polygamists—.
If the common black bird—*Turdus merula*—.
I think we're in this for the long haul. That's
    what someone always says, at the end.

Nine Wild Turkeys in a Field

Come now. Could we have one more day. Have
    one last time. Slowly they shuttled the cut hill.
They did not stop. They did not hurry. The sound
    they made was like broken teeth,
                       like a muttering

inside walls. The big one in back crossing back
    and forth behind the young. Could be sorrow,
the feeling in the breeze, inside the trees, we were feeling.
    She said, what meaneth that, Let the Trees
                       of the Wood

rejoyce? For they were in the trees then, but for
    the big one, in back—the cankered crabs grown sour
along the fence line. Fog was an echo. *Wut meen*
    the treee. It was like a filament, along
                       the fence line,

the fog, and midway up the stubby trees. It was like
    a quiet fire had wept down to wisps but still furling.
We could hear the slow birds stepping on leaves
    or picking at the ground stones
                       just beyond us.

There, in the trees, them going on up the hill.

    You knelt and I dug my heel until a little hole was

there, and you set your Ball jar down, of wildflowers

      in the hole, balanced there; you

                            fluffed them

with your fingers. Got up. Could we have known,

    we might have said more at the time. So

we put flowers down, beside the one cut stone

      named and patient below fog, and the

                         sorrowing trees

there in the field. We called it a field. It was

many things. The big birds passing through.

Gravel

Weed-wrack and wild grape
$\qquad$ hanging from the dusty trees
that touch above the narrow road.
$\qquad$ I'm driving my way back

—rough passage over gravel—
$\qquad$ back the slow miles over
the creek, the lapsed meadow
$\qquad$ we walked for arrow points,

until the road narrows to path.
$\qquad$ I park the car. I pick my step
past rusty barbed wire through
$\qquad$ a clearing to the house.

Back the house. Back the years.
$\qquad$ Back with him now with me
over broken floorboards,
$\qquad$ stone footers, the pot stove—

a whippoorwill, years distant
$\qquad$ through the paneless frames.
Half a staircase leading up
$\qquad$ over the century of beams.

Back now again the old road,

                    disappearing through white woods,
where he lay down and breathed

                    no more.

The Loneliness of Animals

I don't think I know what it feels like
I know I don't   to drag one's self so

slowly "like a zombie" down a cracked
hard, rock-cut creek bed   in Illinois

to be lifted   still churning one's legs
to be the subject of such testing:

to be found to be *Macrochelys*
temminckii   from one's own fine blood-

line, by DNA   of the genus
Chelydra   à la Coenraad Jacob

Temminck "native to a region that
makes up the northernmost end of the

species' range": and now a real shock to
biologist Chris Phillips, who'd been

diving   hoping to find he said one
"male alligator snapping turtle

with a transmitter on its back," last
one precisely   he'd previously

released in the area with hopes
"of spurring population growth":

not this   female   at 22 pounds
"way bigger than expected," spring-like

neck dorsal ridges "like some plated
dinosaur"   so he held her   Ethan

Kessler grad student   just so as he
was taught   for the photo hand behind

her head hand to the side along her
shell-back: ginger   not to lose a thumb

to her steel-trap jaws "the turtle's mouth
is camouflaged, and it possesses

a vermiform (i.e., 'worm-shaped') ap-
pendage at the tip of its tongue   to

lure fish"   by imitating movements
of a worm, "drawing prey to the mouth";

adds Wikipedia   *and they do
not make particularly good pets*:

so when they "reintroduced" her back
into the wild: by which, I think, they

mean dredged rivers drained swamps small wood-runs
culverts check dams and irrigation-

crop-circle-exurbs   her battery-
transmitter died   immediately:

and "finding her in the waters' depths
again might take 30 years." Let's hope so.

Extinction

When you are gone they will read your footprints,
if they still read, as they might a poem about love—
wandering in circles, here and there obscured,
washed out in places by weather, sudden landslide.
Keep walking, pilgrim. This is your great tale.

A slight wrinkle   on the pond   as he said

all that's left of   this life is   what remains

for the next   three redwings   motionless now

atop cattails   are match tips   soon enough

to strike out   this evening on   one black flame—

THREE

Whale Fall

       1.

One dies.
Eschrichtius
       robustus, gray,
       of the sole living genus, of baleen,

of the family
Eschrichtiidae, slate
       gray or darker,
       and notable, now, for

gray-white patterned scars
left by parasites, two
       blowholes "which can
       create a distinctive

V-shaped
blow in calm wind conditions";
       and falls, as
       it falls, as through blue breeze;

and swirls, light
as a tissue, drifting down—
       down, through
       the cool layers, the sifted light

of sea-wind-
warmed currents, loose galaxy
        of whirling flecks, slow-
        motion, in a haze;

in whose first stage, falling,
now, the "mobile
        scavengers" drift alongside,
        sleeper sharks

and thin hagfish
—or, as the book calls them,
        "enrichment opportunists"—
        come to feed

at the soft flanks and fat,
for weeks, as the
        bones grow exposed, all
        of them, spinning down . . .

        2.

We might hear rain before the rain. Sirens.
Hail before it cracked the hundred panes.

Or lay our heads on the desks and listen
to our blood whispering in the woodgrain.

In 1963 the warnings are
piecemeal, part of the good day's play or work.

44

We might need to cover our heads. Hold hands
in the hallway. Look away from the blast.

*

July 29, 2013: a sperm whale found deceased on the beach of
a small island off the coast of the Netherlands had dozens of
plastics bags, nine meters of rope, two long pieces of garden hose,
a couple of flowerpots, and a plastic spray canister in its stomach.

*

I'm watching a hummingbird, bare thumb-
top—gray-green blur—dip to my feeder bulb

and dart off, over the barn, to a wire.
A. colubris. Little serpent. I hear

the burr of wings; and already it's back—
dips again, hovers there; sips now; attacks

the tube of red sugar-water until
bubbles aerate, like an aneurism.

*

June 28, 2016: an 80-foot blue whale (*Balaenoptera musculus*)
caught in 200 feet of fishnet, crab lines, channel buoys off the
coast of Orange County: lines cut through its mouth, wrapped
its fins. "Blue whales are typically thought to be more off-shore

animals, and crabbing gear is thought to be more inshore, but obviously the spatial overlap between those two is coming into conflict," explained Leigh Torres. "The fact that we see this entanglement isn't terribly surprising, though it is unique."

*

Weeks I couldn't sleep. Years I couldn't waken.
I found a note I'd written one ill night.

pines shredded   ice snow
such wind
  rips the night

I run my tongue above my tooth, aching.
And know it's coming back once more. The warning

—right cuspid, gum swollen, puffed as a pea—
two days before the viral fire, the toxic sea . . .

*

March 31, 2016: 13 sperm whales (*Physeter macrocephalus*)
beached themselves off the shallow coast at Tönning, Germany:
"We may never know the exact cause," wrote Danny Groves.
Stomach contents: 43 feet of fishing net, 100 plastic bags,
golf balls, sweatpants, greenhouse glass sheeting, cigarette
butts, hypodermic needles, a plastic car engine cover, a bucket . . .

*

Cottonwood seeds. Gnats' wings in the sunlight.
Whirl of dust motes in the haze of still light.

If it were so simple as to drift down.
If it were so easy as getting up again.

Little bug, little serpent. The air slows
with summer thickness when you fly away.

And the feeder bobs there like a red buoy
on the green waters of a distant bay.

3.

A drawer full of notes. Years trying to—

   all night sweating

                     sheets so heavy   burning—

   600 lymph nodes

                   I know where you live—

She's eighteen months old. *Up, up?* I'm afraid—

   One of my titers read 2560
   "Active." "Acute." "You really are sick."

so weak—to pick her up. I pick her up—

Aggregate allergen: grasses, wheat, milk,
acidics, trees (?): multiple exclusion . . .

Temp 103.7. Good night, moon—

After a sunny walk with her wagon—
next day—   *panting*

                              testicles so swollen
                    freezing

system flushing itself—into the waves—

Aggregate infection: Liver. Kidney.
Heart sac. Spleen. Gut. Urinary tract. Neck . . .

good night, night bird—far off—through the high pines—

        4.

In the second stage,
at 4,000 feet
        (or 122
        "atmospheres"),

weight suspends;
a heavy thing in one world
        floats like willow seed in a breeze
        in this,

a moving vast through
that darkness, silent . . .
        they don't need
        much else—oxygen, nor light—

the frilled shark
and fang-tooth, the spider crab,
        the vampire squid, who strip the dead
        down now

beyond bones
to the merest blueprint of
        whale; slow down-spinning of
        months, a year, more,

the hypotoxic haze,
the "marine snow"
        in a kind
        of afterlife of weather—

drifting down of plankton, and
protists, soot,
        sand, fecal matter in aggregates
        "held

together by a
sugary mucus"—
        all, sifting down,
        through the aphotic zone;

and its vast weight,
once 40-plus tons, skin
      "like a peeled hard-boiled egg,"
      patched with orange

whale lice, white barnacles,
it too long since
      sloughed, shed, dissolving as
      particulate

snowfall, orbital,
in this new galaxy
      of darknesses;
      borne, like seed, floats down . . .

    5.

I have been silent for a long time now.
You know I am serious about the whales.

You don't know this. I floated there in stillness,
in white sheets. White boughs breaking. The pines

in ice and wind like a hammering pulse.
When I woke I couldn't speak or make sense.

And when I slept again I didn't sleep.
And more fires spreading through the body's depths.

*

"Plastic Garbage Patch Bigger Than Mexico Found in Pacific."
National Geographic: These pieces of plastic are not necessarily
floating bottles, bags, and buoys, but "teeny-tiny pieces of plastic
resembling confetti." 90% of sea birds consume it. Over eight million
tons of new plastic trash finding its way into the oceans every year.
The Great Pacific Garbage Patch moves in a clockwise direction,
like a toilet. It circulates an area of 7.7 million square miles.
70% of marine debris sinks to the bottom of the ocean.

New York Times: Plastiglomerate was "discovered" by Charles Moore,
a sea captain, surveying plastic washed up on a remote, polluted
stretch of sand on Hawaii's Big Island. It is a new stone, a fusion
of natural and manufactured materials. "If [plastiglomerates] are
buried within the strata," says Jan Zalasiewicz, an English geologist,
"I don't see why they can't persist in some form for millions of years."

*

You'd think we'd learned enough to duck our heads.
(It's time for arithmetic.) Okay, kids,

who can tell me what you get when you divide
a number by itself? Silence. Overhead

the hum of fluorescents. The swallowing sea
of storm clouds out the window beyond the trees.

What does it take to raise sufficient alarm?
When do you hide? Where do you fly from harm?

*

Aggregates increase "like snow." Aggregation theory represents
a two-state system ["time for chemistry, kids"] . . . to characterize
the formation of marine aggregates and the loss due to sinking:

$$\frac{C}{t} \qquad gC \qquad\qquad \alpha r\; GC$$

where

- C_i is the concentration of the cells
- r is the radius of each cell
- G is the shearing rate
- α is the stickiness coefficient
- g is the growth rate.

Thus, aggregation of marine particles is more prevalent when
cell and particle concentration is higher (e.g., algal blooms).

*

Do the math. That's what the specialist said.
The first doctor winked. Some people just need

to get sick in order to relax. Thanks.
Your T cells go bat-crazy. They attack

the healthy host: it's your immune system
out of control . . . viral opportunism

running rampant through your lymph. It won't stop.
You can't sleep. Flushing toxins down the pipe . . .

*

Wikipedia: marine snow is a variety of mostly organic matter,
including dead or dying animals, and plankton . . . also plant parts
and degrading plant material. Because of the relatively long
residence time of the ocean's thermohaline circulation, carbon
transported as marine snow into the aphotic zone by the biological
pump can remain out of contact . . . for more than a thousand years.

A blue jay lands in the fringe tree. Sudden downfall of petals.

The massive galaxy of matter as the body floats down through
the ocean's zones is granular, a snowy sand, agglomerate of
debris in slow orbit around the disintegrating husk of whale.
Here are the five most common "unnatural" causes of death.
Entanglement. Ship and propeller strikes. Commercial fishing
(i.e., human appetite). Bycatch. Climate change (i.e., global warming).

*

I was sick for years. Now it's coming back.
Little serpent sipping there beyond the deck.

A. colubris. The need for names (my friend
wants to help) is thirst for clarity, affinity.

Yet sometimes I watch the trees. Let the whip
maples weep and go blur above the barn.

Now they're a wash of green, a mere wave.
Now they carry me, as he says, in their arms.

      6.

Viral-capsid antigen: 2410—

    Hummingbird's back again—green bulb blinking
    its alarm.
            Now the first heavy drops . . .

Good night, little one—asleep with her toys—

    Aggregate testing: lymphoma TB
    "tumors?" HIV leukemia Grave's—

Like photons, but slow, around a gray sun—

    And when I blink and bring them back, in their
    distinctions, the silver limbs like water—

"chronic running into walls"   "chronic fog"—

Every second, trillions of neutrinos
passing through your arm, "like you're transparent"—

CFS :: CF/IDS :: ME :: "no kidding?"—

Right. Sperm. Great blue. Minke (common; Antarctic).
Fin. Sei. Humpback. Bryde's. Gray. Orca. Pygmy . . .

Cicada husk hangs on through the hard rain—

     7.

When I pull out my old notes, my notebooks full of shaky words—

In the third stage, a whale fallen through the deepest oceanic zones—

bathyal, abyssal—may take a hundred years—more—to decompose—

When I find the old books, I see checkmarks, dog-ears, underlines—

Full restoration of health is still your hope and expectation, but—

giant isopods—squat lobsters—*Osedax*—sea cucumbers—bristle worms—

You know I am serious about the whales: [*Views of Jeopardy*]—

Born in 1925, in Pittsburgh, PA—with a metro population greater—

than the global population of whales, perhaps less than two million—

When you hear [   ]   it's already [   ] *Shh. Close your eyes*—

Languages are dying at a rate of one every two weeks—

pine pollen, gnats' wings—glints in air—dust motes, mold spore—

this.fucked.flux.lux.crux // (broken piece of lamp garbage)—

Each eye the size of a grapefruit. Heart bigger than a Smart-car—

But what we see is infinitely less than what we don't see. Up, up?—

Cottonwood seed—polymers, i.e., plastic "foam": gas bubbles—

I can't believe I'm getting it again, "you have always"—"such—

darkness"—measured by a billion bioluminescent wanderers—

Wherever you sit is the center of the universe—wherever—you—

Hear the warning it's too late. Flatfish. Time for math again, kids—

polystyrene "*for infant teething*"—biosemiotics: every cell has—

a cognitive element. SnotBot: whale-breath DNA—in decay—

and lived for eighty-seven years—mostly alone—mostly islands—

In the third stage, a whale fallen through the deepest zones—

bathyal, abyssal, down through the coldest depths, may take that—

long to decompose, a hundred years, more—no light—no oxygen—

[What do you mean] [what do we *do* about it]—*shh*—

Think of this one, spinning, *Eschrichtius robustus*, gray, of the—

sole living genus, of baleen, of the family Eschrichtiidae, like a—

tissue, floating in the darkness, to settle there. It takes your life.

FOUR

Elegiac

The moon sets a place for him at the long table.
See how his plate shines among the glittering knives.

A Portrait of My Father in Seven Maps

1.

Here I heard them. Here the big rocks. Here the place
with the tent. Did you cut enough willows for the lines, did
you hang them, are they treble are they single, we'll need
the right hooks for the bait. We walked across water
so cold here it was burning. It was warm. When you
put your slippers on you have to watch your step, the grass
is wet the tiles are wet it's pitched a little down. So here
hold the rod. When you don't know where you are—

2.

In Ptolemy's *Geography* the uncharted is not far away.
   Written in lampblack ink made from soot.
Where is she. Never far beyond Serica beyond
   Sinae nothing the island of Taprobane then nothing and

Aurea Chersonesus. Did you hear them first. Did you
   tie the boat to the willow to a stone. Inscribed on a roll
of papyrus cut from plants growing along the Nile Delta.
   Why have you chosen Ptolemy do you think—

3.

Harry T. Kelsh's patents (1949–55) for the machine
he sat at for a decade—my father, working the arms, tracing
contours with mechanical pencils, with semi-transparent
paper—include photogrammetric plotting, gimbaled

diaphragms for optical projection, stereoscopic projection,
compensator designs for *moving the floating mark of*
the mapping table, instead of the lenses. Hence
the Kelsh machine. He sat me down. To trace a path—

4.

who could find his way
                              in the woods   in the dark

in rainstorm and snow-cover
                              when he fell   the first time

how did they know it
                              he said he was disoriented

who could tell which weed
                              which root some manner of knot

starlings in the blue crab
                              kingfish or jay on a low branch

of bobbing lindens
                    where were you going but

I don't remember that
                    who waited the last night

quietly   still through the long night
                    still holding her hand—

        5.

I am seven or eight. He's about thirty. Keep still now.
Only cartography's general reference map has

the hubris to present the world, you know, *as it really is*,
as if to say now and forever. Ground the heel to a stone,

rock the rod to get your reading when the hash-mark's high.
Who carries me over water to our fire cicadas star-dots among

weeping willows scent of the older herds. Any tree could
be the axis mundi around which the universe turns—

        6.

Here I heard them singing. Marsh wrens. Her singing.
    Let's chalk a path to the dining room. Let's put
a piece of tape on the drain on the floor to the north-point.
    This way we know where we are. His latitude expressed as

climata, the length of the longest day, not degrees of arc.

 It's where we stood. Furrows in a cornfield.

What Ptolemy called chorography was simply a survey.

 It was not the world. He fell from a chair a ladder a tree—

    7.

It's maybe four miles from East Circle to Adams Street Place.

Place being where. Ptolemy's purpose was not to imagine

the whole of natural existence but account for the known edge,

beyond which. He is eighty-eight. I am sixty. Beyond which

we can't see. The arms the pencils his 3-D stereo-glasses

on a table stand. Limestone ledge there's the back way down.

Bring it up slow and check what we caught. Here hold on.

I know where we're going. She heard. I know. We won't be back—

One September

1.

Cicadas have filled the century elm. Filled
    the upper-story down through the shadow depths,
the two hundred thousand leaves, alternate on a branch. Saw-
    toothed, ovate, small as a child's sweet palm.
A great shadow covers the busy corner. Whirr of
    the song cycle, even now, above the traffic, the breeze—

2.

We touch the hand of the child asleep.
    Has her fever broken? Is she still? We say the most
ancient things, even to her sleeping ears. Is she cold?
    Will she remember us? Or not touch at all
for fear of rousing her. Some of our songs without words—.
    Luck is a tree branching to the roof outside

3.

the window overhead, a voice among shadows
    over the busy corner. Over parents now
in SUVs and hatchbacks, bumper-tight at the curb,
    a few bikes propped near the tree, standing around
in our social distances, come to pick up the young from school.
    Some of our songs on transparent, small wings—

4.

We know the age of the tree, *Ulmus parvifolia*,
  from arborists come to draw specimen samples
from its core, to grind down—take its temp,
  said one—for its DNA. Why did this one live, this one, among
the tens of millions broken by disease? By sac fungi.
  Vascular wilt. Lacebark, its other name, our mottled elm—

5.

The young teachers, their handheld megaphones,
  in sundresses, school-color masks, are calling the children
by name for their parents, one by one, the whirr
  and click of doors. Come just in time.
The sound lifts and breathes, like a certain music of the sea,
  if the sea were still here, as it will be, again, in another age—

6.

When did they arrive? The cicadas, I mean.
  Cicadas above us all inside the green shadow. Here's
one, seven or eight, running to her waiting father.
  I can't see their faces. But when he tries to set her down
in his bike's back seat, she sings out, muffled, *no no!*
  She wants—she flaps her arms—to run along behind, and fly,
    soon now—.

Hold Hands

We were in the trees. White curtains opened.
Your shoulders in my hands then your knees
drew upward. Rain like petals there. Rain
like breeze. Now the birds were in the trees
two stories up, our window, where blowing
leaves were level with our sheets. We were
in the street. We were holding hands as hands
were holding us. What hands there were were
where we were. In trees. Our children there
as songbirds were. The hands where we were
in the trees were holding us there. Where we
were in the street. Please the rain to please
the petals in the breeze like rain. Please to
draw your hair along my hands your hands
are holding us. Lines along the window lane
are holding us like songs. As now the songs the
sirens in the trees. Lines along the window lane.
Your hair in feathers where the children are.
Whose curtains singing. Whose hands are
holding us who cry like birds. Hold hands.
The birds are in the trees. The birds our
children there in cages singing in the trees.

Six Hours

1.

His hands are folded and gathered on his chest.
Each arm is a wing in stillness tucked close.

He has laced his fingers loosely over
and under like the strings of good shoes.

2.

Someone has come to check his breathing; tap
the tubes; add a few numbers to the chart.

We might see his father's hands in these hands.
He might hold them for us—pages in a book.

3.

What book? We'd swear he moved. Now someone
has opened a blind and the sun comes wild

with sudden bright splashes over the room,
the side table with its small cup of pills.

4.

He blinks one eye to the warmth. He's resting
with his head on two pillows. Did he smile?

In a poem he calls hands requisite—
for reading, for holding, holding nothing . . .

5.

He looks as though he's holding back breath
from a wound. Or, if he were standing, touching

his heart to see if his pulse were secure.
His hands are still, soft to touch, when we touch,

6.

and dappled with the canker of field crabs
in a yard, in Ohio, in the sun.

The boy in him might pick one and throw it
to scatter those blue jays back into clouds.

We Are Gone

Even the night cooling down is slick with heat.
Even the sheet we share like a humming skin.

From three stories up the sounds of the street,
drinkers at the curb, a wet hiss of dry tires,

is a rhythm through our box fan, like panting.
When we sleep it is piecemeal until morning.

*

Listen, the years are short. They are nothing.
I write each morning, while you are at work.

In the heat of day, I walk to the library, cold
water at the fountain, air-conditioned air; walk

with a new book back in the elm-lined shade.
At night I meet you at the top of the stairs.

*

Where are you gone, who loved me so long
one summer far from home? Days are long.

Even the heat is lovelier there, as memory is.
We make lemonade from powder. Little wonder

the years are less than a breath, like a song
on the radio heard as the rhythm of languor.

*

Whistle of the ice cream truck. Drinkers at the curb.
Days and nights of heat, of sex, such tenderness.

When we sleep sometimes it is to dream of the days.
Where are they gone? Meeting on the stairs,

laughter and light, a small meal, a bottle of wine.
When we wake it is piecemeal, untl we are gone.

We never ended—   *we simply began*

as though we were first   *beneath the cold stars*

of a cloudless sky   *it was never night*

in our other places   in the small brain

of extinct summer   *let us be like beaks*

among dark berries   *along ancient boughs*

even now the clocks   *in their feather gloves*

are measuring space   *for the new graveyards—*

FIVE

Echolocation

1.

In our year of distances—*O, nie płacz, nie*—I listen for voices—
                              Are you there?
Katie at the shore of a great lake. Page to the east—

In a village by the sea. Out my window the hummingbirds whir—
                              Barn to feeder
to bough. We are thin wires. FaceTime. Skype—

96° today. Ruby-throats bumping each other. Bunting each other—
                              Off the feeder.
Littlest songbirds, doubling their weight for the trip—

                    *

There's a story about a hummingbird, riding the back of other—
                              Birds on its
long migration. 500 miles just to cross the Gulf—

Have you heard? Over the long lawn of a green sea, under which—
                              Great bodies of
whales pass, like shadows—the ancient Cambrian sea—

Dawn Upshaw, in Górecki's Third, lento y largo. *No matter what—*
                              I'm doing,
it slows me in my tracks, to drift there, in the sway—

                    *

When I heard it the first time, I had to pull my truck off the highway—
                              Ohio 15, near
Findlay, to write in the margin of my sad map, quick—

As I could—*Gereshy something something*—what I heard the DJ say—
                              Years later
I read he used monastic laments, Polish folktales—

In the great green room there was a telephone. Good night, moon—
                              Now to touch
the light switch. Good night, light. Now a wall—

                    *

Graffiti from a Gestapo prisoner. A little girl, Helena Błażusiakówna—
                              Etched her
prayer to Mary in a cell at Zakopane, so the high A♭—

Cuts through the black abyss. *Music is continuous; only listening—*
                              Is intermittent.
Jean Valentine quoting John Cage (mis)quotes Thoreau—

The smaller the bird the faster the wings. They shouldn't work—
                                    Ten feathers,
like cellophane. Flying upright, facing the world—

    2.

In our year of distances. It's why I've called tonight—*among—*
                                    A steady storm
of correspondences. Among the cluttering noises—

Listen. There are three of them. Far, off the San Benito islands—
                                    What started as
a sound. A new species, swimming there all this time—

Waves, in both directions along the string, reinforcing—
                                    And canceling
each other—to form a responding harmonic—

               *

Of the family Ziphiidae. Of beaked whales, whose fossils date—
                                    To the Miocene.
15 million years ago. *We heard something—*

That doesn't match, visually or acoustically, anything we've—
                                    Known to
exist. Beaked whales, deep divers, down to 1,600 feet—

Researchers estimate the lowest frequency sounds of a whale—
                              Can travel
as far as 10,000 miles without losing their energy—

                    *

Are you there? Do you know I am here? *O, nie płacz, nie—*
                              I have
called to tell you, simply, there are whales—

Deepest midnight. I have called to say there are whales as—
                              Old as stones,
yet new to us, among the winds, in our world—

The movement is resolved when the strings hold a chord—
                              Without di-
minuendo for nearly one and a half minutes—

                    *

Among storms and pestilence, the stupor of the day. And when—
                              The midnight rain,
or raking snow, or stillness only rips the black abyss—

There are wings too thin for theory, carrying songs across this world—
                              Listen. Tell me
what you hear. Tell me, before we sleep, once more—

We are a shape the wind makes in these leaves as it passes through—
                                        We are a shape
the wind makes in these leaves, passing through—

This Morning

1.

The dusty one flies back to the viburnum.
She hops a ladder of shoots from the base
to the higher tangle, where her nest is—shred of
brown leaf in her beak, needle of pine, slim twig.
The bright one sits above in the lilac tree.
He watches from the weathervane over the barn.
He's the alarmist, the red bobber on a creek,
when the dusty one flies back to the viburnum.

2.

And the peonies in shadow, peonies in sun
go on opening their lavish blooms, swaying there,
bending to the heaviness of their blossoming.
Their inadequate stems. Their slender stems.
Beside the viburnum they bow, and ants grow busy
lifting sugar from the cracked buds, unspooling
each bobbin of petals. What can hold them all?
The peonies in shadow, peonies in sun—

3.

I have so much to account for. Shame and sorrow.
I wish I had thought to put my face to the grass.
Yet there is no hurry in my friend's voice
when the fox slips back into her woods.
What is down there? Viburnum burning—
and below, a few torn blossoms dotted
with mites and the grass still slick with dew.
I have so much to account for, shadow and shame.

4.

There is no hurry in my friend's voice, nor
the cardinals stitching a breeze, warming their eggs.
I wish I had spoken when it mattered, but who
can know each time when to call or keep still?
The bright one watches from the lilac tree,
and a new peony opens to morning—big as
a softball—so heavy it falls to the grass.
The dusty one flies back to the viburnum.

Four Poses

You bend your foot, slow as the heron at hunt,
who shifted to the sun side of the shoulder

to let us pass yesterday beneath those reedy capers.
It flew, when it flew, wispy as a reed. Cocked

stiletto orange beak, a great white bulb-
body glistening into wings. Ardeidae, of the

species *Ardea alba*—you hardly seem to move—
it was like a crane, but closer in relation to the pelican,

common enough in these parts. Now you
are the skier—looking out the big glass to the bay,

the bright water we love, wing-tipped, white-
capped, depending, wild or serene as each cloud.

You crouch and hold; and the algae bloom,
come so far—from the Amazon, some say, some

thousand miles, a species a billion years old—floats
in its ribbon locked in a gyre beyond our shore.

Sahara dust pinks the sky at nightfall.
So still the stars, yet whirling in a gyre, too . . .

Now the brown millipede that fell from the sky,
you said, to the red tiles outside our door,

curled there come morning like a palm frond.
Gongolo, a local name. *A. monilicornis* in

the taxonomy. How many legs. Oh, how slow.
Among the oldest known animals on land.

When you look up finally from these stillnesses,
you are the heron once again. The millipede

curling to the press of sun.
                              Now you are the sun.

The Bathers at Nerja

Their pleasure is their memory. Water.
The bird song body alert but at rest.
There had been war; peace. There had
been war. Some walked straight
into the waves, some waited on shore,
tamping down towels, shading their brows.
Chiffchaffs flipped down from the scrub
to pick at the seaweed; little ringed plovers
tipped along the snarling lips of the waves.
When a parasailer floated closer offshore
than he should have, probably, higher,
hanging above them like a toy, did some
remember the soldiers who once dropped
from those heights, the gray puffs
of their chutes, landing, tumbling,
running the grass like a terrible wind?
Look at those two, sitting off by themselves,
sharing grapes, a thermos. White gulls.
Is memory a blessing, as we say?
One stands to wave at shadows in a boat
slowly passing by, waving, waving back—
but hello, go away, who can tell?

Thirty-Six Silos

To make a harvest of loneliness. To intend it.
Since the fields are green. Since the fields are tall—

You walk into black shucks, forty years by.
Shoving your way through the stiff, sharp leaves—

Where is the car, where are the lights, whose house.
Whetting their long blades all night-wind—

The cows were out. Corn trampled. Hard rain.
And then, hard storm, the Air Force came to latch the gates—

Once she said be gone. Said where is your sorrow.
One by one, or twos or threes, there in the black fields—

The world opens a pair of eyes to look at itself.
How many did you hit? Three or four. One down there—

Ground ear corn: 1.94 cubic feet/bushel at 15.5% moisture.
Johnson has a locust growing through a dome now—

We got farm stacks all over. We got missile stacks below.
He had 300 acres of corn. Don't.

Now a field of tares—

What do you smell? Time. Oh please, don't get poetic.
The farther they stretch the smaller you grow down—

Farm silos upward of 200 feet. Wheat, woodchips, ferment.
Minuteman, Atlas, Titan. Down 150 feet x 55 feet wide—

How could they take care of nuclear missiles.
And not remember to check the gates? Blame thunder—

When you come back out, endlessness of wind blowing.
From the start of time to be swept through one's ribs—

Airbnb. *Missile Silo Fixer-Upper Now Swanky Bachelor Pad*.
Military latrine; farmer's storage bin; "ultimate" safe room—

Pick your poison. Plutonium-239 half-life 24,000 years.
Uranium-235, 700,000,000. Uranium-238, 4.5 billion—

Now a branch and now a nightingale. I'm begging.
Now a tongue and now the words for tongue—

Skunk cabbage, field bindweed, pig wort, did I say.
Sorrow, did you say more, how long till we know—

The stars above are dots in a clattering wind.
Leaving the broken car. Walking alone in the field—

Now a silo reaching up to the black earth of sky—
Now a silo burning with the half-life of the sun—

So Far

Well we got out of the car. The gravel there.
Gravel along the way, gravel over black tar,
it going with us. Picked up the little creek
at the fallow cornfield, and chicory all along
the way, blue-eyed and wild. Queen Anne's lace
among it. Thistle among it. We went on there.

It going with us. Until those birds, circling,
and the bridge reaching up, rust of the trestle
cresting the brown sky. You went on there
under the low girders, the wood side-beams,
where you looked down one way. Brown
tug of the waters below. Well I went there

too, and we kicked a spit of gravel
down a drain-hole, spatter in the water.
When she died, did she know you? More
of the swallows up from the slats wherever
the gravel splashed. Circling now
above us. I don't think she knew you.

Well she gripped my two fingers
hard, the old way. She seemed to smile.
Slatted road-boards below us, to see

through, to the brown water, and look,
two or three gar drifting slow with
the current too, shadows with teeth

really, below the surface not far.
More birds calling down the way, where
the water turned maybe a quarter mile.
It going with us. Well this is where we
dropped her in. Dropped her in. Urn made
out of salt. She wanted to be that way,

ashes writ in water. So you say. You
there in the whisper. The birds sunk into
some limbs' hollowing green shadow.
When I die, will you be there? Will you
watch me go? Turned back for the car.
Her going with us. Having flowed so far.

It doesn't take much   only a little

the cottonwood seeds   in fluffs like white foam

upon green waters   seeming to sail back

to slender branch-tips   that only seconds

before let them go   on the waving breeze

when have you felt so   moved as they are moved

and to whom to what—

Acknowledgments

These poems first appeared in the following publications, to whose editors I extend my grateful acknowledgment. *The American Poetry Review*: "Middle Devonian," "Turner's Clouds for Plumly," and *"We never ended"*; *Bennington Review*: "Echolocation" and "Sensationalism"; *Copper Nickel*: "Elegiac"; *The Eloquent Lyric* (Persea Books): *"Is there no sound to"*; *The Georgia Review*: "Mullein" and "This Morning"; *The Kenyon Review*: "Four Poses"; *Michigan Quarterly Review*: "The Bathers at Nerja," "The Loneliness of Animals," and "So Far"; *The Nation*: "Extinction"; *The New England Review*: "Hold Hands," "Nine Wild Turkeys in a Field," and "Storm Psalm"; *The New York Times*: "Hold Hands"; *The New Yorker*: "We Are Gone"; *Poem-a-Day* (Academy of American Poets): "Gravel"; *Poetry*: "Nineteen Spikes," "Snow Falling," and "Whale Fall"; *Raritan*: *"It doesn't take much,"* "One September," "Six Hours," and "The Telling"; *The Yale Review*: "A Portrait of My Father in Seven Maps," *"A slight wrinkle,"* and "Thirty-Six Silos."

I am grateful also to Denison University for years of support and encouragement, and to Jill Bialosky for her guidance, care, and custody.

Notes

In addition to quotations I've attributed directly in my poems, I have echoed or reused phrases and information from other sources, as noted here.

EPIGRAPH

The epigraph to this book is from W. S. Merwin's "My Brothers the Silent" from *The Lice* (1967).

"NINETEEN SPIKES"

"Farmer Dies Trapped in Grain Bin," *Columbus Dispatch*, May 29, 2013; "Barn," CERN Writing Guidelines on Nuclear Testing; Stan Tekiela's *Trees of Ohio: Field Guide* (2004); Colin Tudge's *The Tree* (2006).

"TURNER'S CLOUDS FOR PLUMLY"

Stanley Plumly's "Cancer" and "The Jay" from *Orphan Hours* (2012) and "Constable's Clouds for Keats" from *The Marriage in the Trees* (1997); Plumly's *Elegy Landscapes: Constable and Turner and the Intimate Sublime* (2018). I refer to an episode on April 11, 1819, when Keats and Coleridge met briefly while walking at Hampstead Heath; Keats's account is from a letter to his brother George, and Coleridge's less effusive version comes from a conversation with his walking companion Dr. Joseph Henry Green and from his own *Table Talk*. Keats's comment about "lung-blood" is from a letter to Charles Brown.

"Storm Psalm"

Geoffrey Hill's "To William Corbett" from *Canaan* (1998); Psalm 29 and Psalm 119 from *The Bay Psalm Book* (1640); Christopher Smart's *Jubilate Agno* (1759–63, published 1939).

"Is there no sound to"

W. S. Merwin's "The Sound of It" from *Garden Time* (2016).

"Sensationalism"

Larry Levis's "La Strada" from *The Darkening Trapeze* (2016) and "Slow Child with a Book of Birds" from *The Widening Spell of the Leaves* (1991); Dallas Lore Sharp's *Where Rolls the Oregon* (1914). This poem is dedicated to Larry Levis.

"Nine Wild Turkeys in a Field"

Linda Gregerson's "The Day-Breaking If Not the Full Sun Shining on the Progresse of the Gospel in New-England" from *Waterborne* (2002); Jos Charles's "IX" from *feeld* (2018).

"The Loneliness of Animals"

Lisa Sheppard, "Team Finds First Wild Alligator Snapping Turtle in Illinois Since 1984," University of Illinois News Bureau, November 13, 2017.

Charles Wright's "Heaven's Eel" from *Caribou* (2014).

"WHALE FALL"

Information and phrases about "whale fall" and "marine snow" are from
entries on those subjects in Wikipedia.

In section two the first prose paragraph derives from an article "7
Strange Things Swallowed by Whales," Brooks Hays, MentalFloss.
com, March 13, 2014; the second paragraph derives from "Rescuers
Try to Save Giant Blue Whale Trapped in Fishing Gear," Aaron Sidder,
NationalGeographic.com, June 28, 2016; the third paragraph derives
from "Sperm Whales Found Full of Car Parts and Plastics," Wajeeha
Malik, NationalGeographic.com, March 31, 2016.

A phrase in section three echoes *Goodnight Moon* (1947) by Margaret Wise
Brown, and a phrase in part four and a sentence in part five (repeated
in part seven) are from "It May Be No One Should Be Opened" by Jack
Gilbert, *Views of Jeopardy* (1962).

In section five the first paragraph is paraphrased from "Plastic Gar-
bage Patch Bigger Than Mexico Found in Pacific," Shaena Montanari,
NationalGeographic.com, July 25, 2017; the second paragraph para-
phrases and takes a phrase from "Future Fossils: Plastic Stone,"
Rachel Nuwer, NewYorkTimes.com, June 9, 2014. In this section the
aggregate theory and formula and the third paragraph on marine
snow are from Wikipedia's article on "marine snow." A sentence here
derives from Stanley Plumly's "Early Nineteenth-Century English
Poetry Walks," *Against Sunset* (2016).

In section seven, one phrase and information on CF/IDS/ME come from
Jesse A. Stoff and Charles R. Pellegrino, *Chronic Fatigue Syndrome: The
Hidden Epidemic* (1988), and Edmund Blair Bolles, *Learning to Live with*

Chronic Fatigue Syndrome (1990); one line comes from Evelyn Reilly's
Styrofoam (2009); details about plastic foam and polystyrene come from
Lynn Keller, *Recomposing Ecopoetics: North American Poetry of the Self-
Conscious Anthropocene* (2018); and the line about language extinction
comes from *Ekopoetyka/Ecopoética/Ecopoetics* by Julia Fiedorczuk and
Gerardo Beltrán (2015).

"A Portrait of My Father in Seven Maps"

Information and phrasing on Ptolemy and his cartography is from Jerry
Botton's *A History of the World in 12 Maps* (2014); information on Harry
T. Kelsh and his plotting machine comes from patent papers he filed,
mainly "Compensating Means for Photogrammetric Instruments" (1955).

"One September"

Stanley Plumly's "Valentine" from *Summer Celestial* (1983).

"Six Hours"

Stanley Plumly's "The Art of Poetry" from *The Marriage in the Trees* (1997).

"*We never ended*"

W. S. Merwin's "Now and Again" from *The Moving Target* (1963).

"Echolocation"

A phrase in Polish from Henryk Górecki's Symphony No. 3 (1977),
also known as the Symphony of Sorrowful Songs; Margaret Wise
Brown, *Goodnight Moon* (1947); Jean Valentine's "Bury Your Money"
from *Shirt in Heaven* (2015); Theodore Roethke's "In a Dark Time"
from *Collected Poems of Theodore Roethke* (1963); Jack Guy, "New
Whale Species Discovered in Mexico," CNN, December 9, 2020;

Jack Gilbert's "Music Is in the Piano Only When It Is Played" from *Refusing Heaven* (2005).

"This Morning"

Jane Hirshfield's "Three Foxes by the Edge of the Field at Twilight" from *The Lives of the Heart* (1997).

"Thirty-Six Silos"

Jack Gilbert's "The Manger of Incidentals" from *Refusing Heaven* (2005); Mark Doty's *What Is the Grass: Walt Whitman in My Life* (2020); Chidiock Tichborne's "[My prime of youth is but a frost of cares]" (1586); Federico García Lorca's "Fragment of a Dark Love Sonnet" from *Poet in Spain* (2017, translation by Sarah Arvio).